BUILDING BLOCKS OF COMPUTER SCIENCE

DEBUGGING

Written by Echo Elise González

Illustrated by Graham Ross

WORLD BOOK

a Scott Fetzer company
Chicago

World Book, Inc.
180 North LaSalle Street
Suite 900
Chicago, Illinois 60601
USA

For information about other World Book publications,
visit our website at **www.worldbook.com**
or call **1-800-WORLDBK (967-5325).**
For information about sales to schools and libraries,
call 1-800-975-3250 (United States),
or 1-800-837-5365 (Canada).

Library of Congress Cataloging-in-Publication Data
for this volume has been applied for.

Building Blocks of Computer Science
ISBN: 978-0-7166-2883-5 (set, hc.)

Debugging
ISBN: 978-0-7166-2890-3 (hc.)

Also available as:
ISBN: 978-0-7166-2898-9 (e-book)

1st printing August 2020

STAFF

Executive Committee
President: Geoff Broderick
Vice President, Finance: Donald D. Keller
Vice President, Marketing: Jean Lin
Vice President, International Sales:
    Maksim Rutenberg
Vice President, Technology: Jason Dole
Director, Editorial: Tom Evans
Director, Human Resources: Bev Ecker

Editorial
Manager, New Content: Jeff De La Rosa
Writer: Echo Elise González
Proofreader: Nathalie Strassheim

Digital
Director, Digital Product Development:
    Erika Meller
Digital Product Manager: Jon Wills

Graphics and Design
Sr. Visual Communications Designer:
    Melanie Bender
Coordinator, Design Development and
    Production: Brenda B. Tropinski
Sr. Web Designer/Digital Media Developer:
    Matt Carrington

Acknowledgments:
Art by Graham Ross/The Bright Agency
Series reviewed by Peter Jang/Actualize
    Coding Bootcamp

TABLE OF CONTENTS

Pesky bugs!................................... 4

Finding bugs................................... 6

Fixing bugs................................... 10

Syntax errors...................................12

Logic errors...................................22

Preventing bugs...................................26

Glossary................................... 30

Go online 31

Index 32

There is a glossary on page 30. Terms defined in the glossary
are in type **that looks like this** on their first appearance.

PESKY BUGS!

TAPPITY TAP

ERROR

HUH!

RROR

Hi! I'm a computer programming mistake, also called a computer bug.

Most people call me Bug!

```
class CHelloWorldApplication : public CEikApplication
    {
    public:
        TUid AppDllUid() const;
    protected:
        CApaDocument* CreateDocumentL();

    };
```


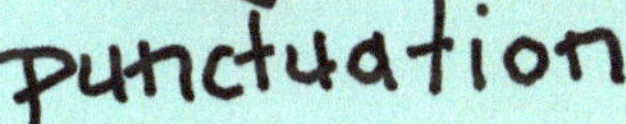
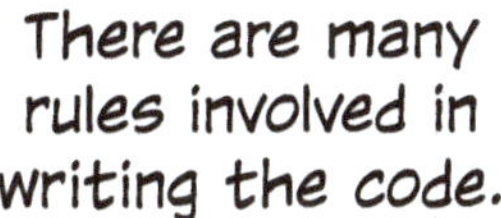

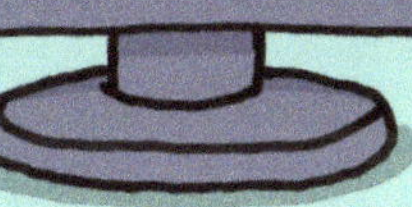

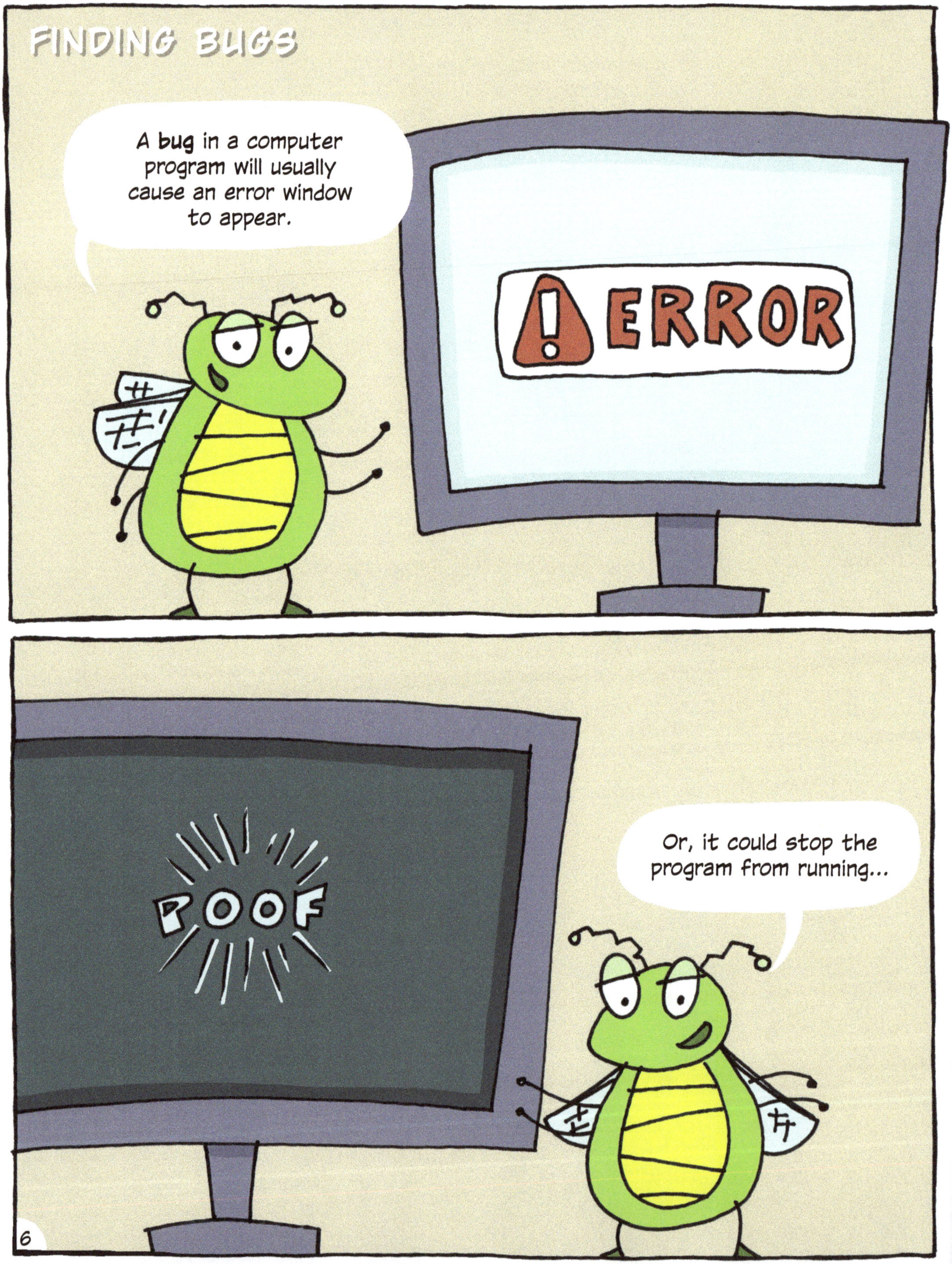

A **bug** in a computer program will usually cause an error window to appear.

ERROR

POOF

Or, it could stop the program from running...

Or cause the program to run improperly.
Once it's clear that there is a problem with the program...
It's up to the programmer to find the bug!

Finding a bug can be tricky.
It can take a long time.

But finding bugs is an important step to fixing them and making a good program.

index.js simple-node X
VARIABLES
8 async init ( ) {
9   const result-axis
10   .get('${AFI_BASE}
11   .then(response =>{
12   response date results
13   console log(item)
14   //update the lamp
15   });
16 }
DEBUG CONSOLE
response: Object
data: Object
results: Array
0: Object {id: 1, price: 12}
1: Object {id: 2, price: 20}
To find a bug, a programmer uses a special program called a debugger.

8   async init ( ) {
9   const result_axis
        ${API_BASE}/setColor
        (response ⇒ {
        ponse.data results
13   console.log(item);
A debugger runs through the program's code line by line while the program is running.

8   async init ( ) {
9   const result_axis
10   get ('${API_BASE}/setColor
11   .then (response ⇒ {
12   response.data.results
13   console log(item),
This process is called stepping.

The programmer can see each line of code as the debugger steps through them one by one.

Because the program is also running, the programmer can see the point when an error happens.

ERROR

The debugger lets the programmer see which line of code is running when the error occurs.
response : Object
  data : Object
    results : Array
      0 : Object {id: 1, price: 12}
      1 : Object {id: 2, price: 20}

FIXING BUGS
The next step in dealing with a **bug** is fixing it!
Thankfully, this is often the easiest part of the process.
Fixing a bug can be simple.
print "HelloWorld*
print "HelloWorld"
Sometimes, the programmer just has to replace an incorrect symbol with the correct one...
10

"Hello World" print
...Or put words or lines of code in the correct order.
print "Hello World"
Sometimes, the solution is a bit more complex.
TAP
TAP
print "Hey World"
print "How are you today?"
It might involve making big changes so that the result of the program better matches the programmer's intention.
It all depends on the kind of bug that needs to be fixed...

There are many different kinds of **bugs** that can occur during coding.
Some bugs occur when code does not follow the rules of the **programming language** being used.

The rules of a programming language are called **syntax**.
SYNTAX

These pretty are flowers?

These flowers are pretty!

In programming, syntax includes putting words in the correct order and using the correct symbols.

Using the wrong word or symbol in a line of code is a common mistake.
RRORE

This kind of mistake can cause a syntax error.
ERROR

A **bug** can happen when a programmer uses a word or symbol that is not part of the **programming language** they are using.

If the word or symbol is not part of the programming language, then the computer cannot recognize it.

TOKEN ERROR

Computer programmers call this a **token error**.

A token error is a kind of **syntax error**.

Here are steps for planting a plant.

Step 3 contains the wrong word!

We can fix this by replacing the wrong word, *boots*, with the correct word, *roots*, in this step.

1. Grab the ?carrot> leaves, close to the $oil.
2. %Jiggle the carrot to l++sen it.
3. Pull the c^rrot out of ### the #soil

1. Grab the ?carrot > leaves, close to the $oil.
2. %Jiggle the carrot to l++sen it
3. Pull the c^rrot out of ### the #soil

1. Grab the carrot leaves, close to the soil.
2. Jiggle the carrot to loosen it.
3. Pull the carrot out of the soil.

Now that we have identified the bugs in the carrot-pulling steps, we can fix them right up.

I'm going to follow these steps to ride a horse.
1. Put on your riding boots.
2. Put on your.
3. Put the saddle on the horse.
4. Get on the horse.
5. Signal the horse to move forward.

I'm stuck on step 2! It doesn't make sense to me!
It seems like there's a word missing here...
A missing word or symbol can sometimes stop a computer from carrying out the program.
1. Put on your riding boots.
2. Put on your.
3. Put the saddle on the horse.
4. Get on your horse.
5 Signal the horse to move forward.

When that happens, the programmer has to find the line of code where the word or symbol is missing and fill it in.

1. Bait the fishing to the attach hook.

2. Your into the water cast line.

3. Bite a fish to wait for.

4. In fish, it bites when a reel!

1. Attach the bait to the fishing hook.

2. Cast your line into the water.

3. Wait for a fish to bite.

4. When a fish bites, reel it in!!

1. Climb the ladder.
2. Pick the low apples.
3. Set a ladder against the tree.
4. Pick the higher apples.

But the result is not quite what we wanted!

In coding, this kind of bug is known as a **logic error**.

Unlike **syntax errors**, logic errors often do not stop the program from running.

Instead, the computer will run the program all the way through, but the result will be different than the programmer intended.

Let's fix this logic error bug by putting the steps in the correct order.

1. Pick the low apples.
2. Set a ladder against the tree.
3. Climb the ladder.
4. Pick the higher apples.

Much better!

1. Sprinkle dog food in the fishbowl.
2. Walk the chickens.
3. Let the cat out of the coop.
4. Brush the fish.

A variable is a piece of information, like a word, that can be changed in the program.

In each of these instructions, the type of pet is a variable.

1. Sprinkle <u>fish</u> food in the fish bowl.

2. Walk the <u>dog</u>.

3. Let the <u>chickens</u> out of the coop.

4. Brush the <u>cat</u>.

It looks like the wrong variables were entered!

PREVENTING BUGS

It's important for programmers to test the code that they write.

Testing code can help them to see problems that might come up.

It also helps to take it slow while coding. It's easy to make a mistake when rushing!

✓ SLOW
✗ RUSHING

It can also help to write your code in as simple a way as possible.

Programmers think about the simplest and most straightforward way to achieve a goal.

When code is written simply, there's less of it, and less opportunity for error.

SIMPLE

Finding a **bug** in your program does not mean that you are a bad programmer.

Every programmer finds a bug sometimes...

#1 Coder
CHAMPION
Even those who are really good at coding...

Even those who have been coding for a long time!

It's natural to make mistakes.

With practice, you can get really good at preventing bugs...

Finding them when they do happen...

And fixing them!

GLOSSARY

bug an error in a program's code that keeps the program from working the way it is intended.

coding language (see programming language)

debugger a program made to find bugs in the code of another program.

logic error a bug that does not stop the program from working but causes it to do the wrong thing.

programming language a set of symbols and rules that programmers use to write computer programs.

stepping the process of using a debugger to check a program's code line-by-line.

syntax the rules that make up the "grammar" of a programming language.

syntax error a bug caused by improper syntax in the code.

token error a bug caused when code includes a word or symbol not in the programming language.

variable a value, or piece of information, that can change.

GO ONLINE

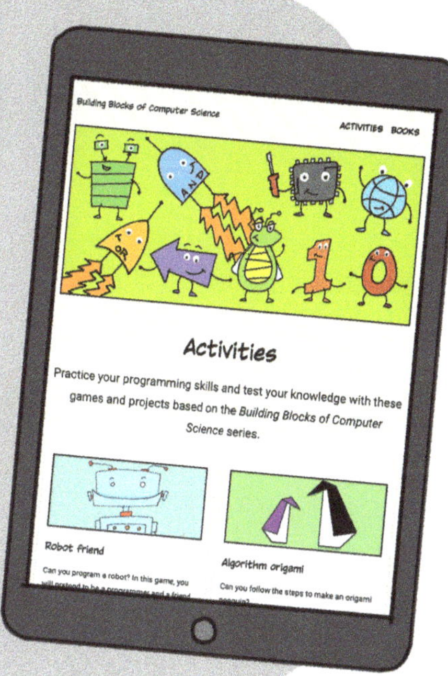

Building Blocks of Computer Science
ACTIVITIES BOOKS
Activities
Practice your programming skills and test your knowledge with these games and projects based on the Building Blocks of Computer Science series.
Robot friend
Can you program a robot? In this game, you will pretend to be a programmer and a friend
Algorithm origami
Can you follow the steps to make an origami

Want to try out
your debugging skills?
Go to this website and
click on the Syntax
Scramble activity!
Check out the other
fun computer science
activities and games, too!

www.worldbook.com
/BuildingBlocks

INDEX

bugs, 4-5; finding, 6-9; fixing, 10-11;
    preventing, 26-27

computer bugs. *See* bugs

debugger, 8-9

errors: logic, 23-25; programming,
    5, 9, 17; punctuation, 5; syntax,
    13-14, 23; token, 14, 16

stepping, 9
syntax, 5, 12-13

testing code, 27

variables, 25